Table of contents

v.   INTRODUCTION

1   I.   CHRISTIAN MINDSETS ON THE MEDIA

9   II.   GETTING TO KNOW THE MONSTER

16   III.   GOSPEL MARKS FOR THE MEDIA

19   IV.   A GOSPEL WAY OF RELATING

27   V.   A GOSPEL WAY OF SEEING

33   VI.   A GOSPEL WAY OF MEASURING

39   VII.   THE GREAT OBJECTIVITY DEBATE

47   VIII.   MAKING IT HAPPEN

APPENDICES

55   I.   Advice on approaching the media

56   II.   Local exercises in media analysis

58   III.   Some questions about objective photography

59   IV.   A case study in objective reporting

62   V.   The Glion communication guidelines

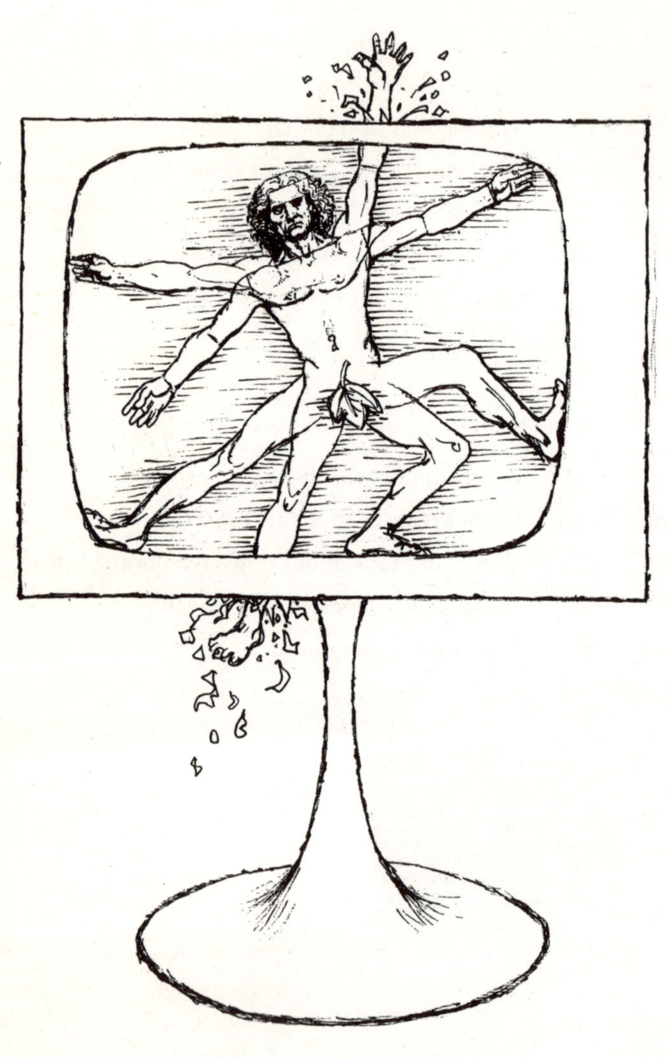

Introduction

in which I say what I'm trying to do, confess some unrepented affections, and suggest that the media provides a prayer book for the secular city.

A late night movie on television, taken slowly with a can of beer. A crisply written newspaper story that brings the feel and smell of an event a world away right onto my breakfast table. A vivid piece of magazine journalism that opens up the excitement of someone else's life, to be read when my own is running flat and slow. Interviews with oil sheiks or cat fanciers, documentaries on battery hens or the next election. The high prose of indignant editorials or the deflating point of a cartoonist's pen — the media is bread, butter and jam for me, an endless source of irritation, education, inspiration and satisfaction, even if it's only from the knowledge that someone else sees the world (or suffers it) in a way I can recognize.

For most of my life, I've been immersed in the media as consumer and producer, as addicted reader, viewer, listener, then amateur journalist, editor, broadcaster with varying degrees of professional pretension. So I write about the media with little or no detachment. The nearest I've ever come to standing back far enough to see it whole is when I arrived here in French-speaking Switzerland from New Zealand to work as an editor for the World Council of Churches. And as my five year-old son keeps reminding me, we forgot to bring our English-speaking television set, so for any really intelligible contact with the world beyond the Alps, we have to rely on an over-priced and very foreign foreign press.

So reliance on the media evaporated overnight. And after surviving the withdrawal symptoms of that deprivation, I've resolved to use my time in isolation to analyse why the media had become such an all-consuming interest, before I get caught in its grips again when I return to the dry ground of an English-speaking culture.

The reports that do filter through into my Swiss enclave suggest there is ever greater alarm and despondency about what the media is doing to our morals and our manners and our minds. I don't believe a tenth of it is true but I do resent the media even attempting to tell me what to do and who to be, all the while pretending that it's only trying to sell me soap or pass on the news of the day.

This modest book is an attempt to look the media in the eye, examine the nature of the beast, then suggest that Christians may well have something creative to say about the state of affairs in the communication industry, by way of both critique and alternative.

For even as we go to press the UNESCO debate on press freedom and responsibility takes on a new intensity. The churches' voice is strangely quiet on the issues involved, critical though they are to all our other social justice concerns. The pages that follow may help to break that silence by sketching some of the starting points that a Gospel perspective provides for the UNESCO debate.

The point of writing consciously as a Christian, however, is not to attempt yet another "theology of the media". Such attempts are too often as abstract as they are banal, making great play of the fact that "in the beginning was the Word... and the Word was God".* The metaphor may have been striking once but we've exhausted its power by using it glibly as a divine endorsement for the enthusiasms of our own prose. The Word is undoubtedly a much more relentless editor than we give him or her credit for.

Worse still, much media theologizing is divorced from the way that print and pictures are actually assembled for broadcast and publication. The realities of deadlines and printers unions, alcoholic journalists and prima donna reporters are conspicuously absent from most church assessments of the press.

So our commentaries will have to be better incarnated if they are going to convince anyone except ourselves. And

---

* All biblical references are taken from the *Common Bible*, Revised Standard Version. London: Collins, 1973.

they'll have to take much closer account of the fact that nude centre spreads, sensational headlines and simplistic exposés are created not only by the greed for easy profits but also by a public need for an understanding of life that can give meaning without waiting, security without struggle and satisfaction without pain.

For millions of people today, the movie theatre is the chapel of the secular city and the newspaper is the Book of the Law. On the radio these people hear their psalms of praise, and through the readers' letters pages, they make their intercessions.

If that imagery seems entirely overstretched, then this book is probably not for you because in my attempt to affirm a Christian's freedom from the media's power, I have to confess how far I have already succumbed to that power. And it would be dishonest to claim I'm totally contrite about that.

For not all the values that the media has helped to form in me are bad, not all the experiences it's invited me to share are negative. What I want to do is not give it up but understand and control it more effectively and learn to laugh at it more readily.

MEDIA

I. Christian mindsets on the media

in which the devil is given his due, we speculate on why clean-up-the-media campaigns backfire, invoke the authority of the Incarnation, cast some old-fashioned pessimism on electronic optimism and share an "I was a media victim" story.

Opinions on the mass media are expressed with the ease of a conversation about football scores. Every second person has heard of someone else's story of misquotation and misrepresentation, or a letter to the editor that was unjustly ignored. Gossip about the media has an allure all of its own and it finds a ready audience in church circles hungry to find blame for or explain away the evils of the day. Here, then, are two schools of media opinion and a brief commentary on each. The proponents of each school can't be neatly divided into liberal and conservative camps for the two attitudes are often found in the same people, left, right and centre, welded together in a schizophrenic mix.

The devil made it — let's blame it

For those who believe that western society is growing permissively out of hand, the media is a favourite whipping boy. So a glimpse of bare breasts on television becomes a promise of sexual anarchy and a cops-and-robbers shootout makes violent anarchy inevitable. But the attempts by social scientists to verify such simple patterns of cause and effect have produced disappointing results for clean-up-the-media campaigners, and our law courts are still refusing to lay legal responsibility for society's woes at the feet of television network and newspaper proprietors.

The sad truth is that whatever horrors the media may hold up as models before us, there are no evils as evil as those we are already capable of. Jesus said the same thing more profoundly when he told the Pharisees that it's the things coming out of a person, rather than the things going in, that we ought to be worrying about. "There is nothing outside a man which by going into him can defile him" (Mk 7 : 15).

To be a mass instrument of *mass* appeal, the media must spend most of its energy on telling us things we already know about ourselves and our world. It works most successfully as a mirror, helping us see what already is. And if we can't recognize immediately the image it holds up, chances are its ratings and sales will slump. Instant recognition is the electronic (and the offset) order of the day.

Despite all the unscrupulous ethics and economics behind the choice and style of so much media coverage, if it didn't have such widespread and immediate appeal, it wouldn't sell.

That appeal is continually underestimated by church groups campaigning against media vices. The effect of such campaigning is often no more than putting fresh dressings on our own weeping sores.

And even when media censorship of morally offensive material does succeed, it frequently builds up a counter-productive effect. Consider the crop of movies from Hollywood in the 1920's, dressed up as biblical sagas, yet reliant on the prurient appeal of repressed sex and violence.

These films emerged at precisely the time that censorship was developed in the California movie capital with the help of the Hays office and church groups. The lure of the "forbidden fruit" mystique proved just as, if not more, powerful an attraction as the explicit portrayal of sex and sin on the screen.

The attempts of morally worthy campaigners to clean up the media so frequently misfire, not because they don't take their cause seriously enough, but because they define it too narrowly. Moral worth is held up as the basis for a whole assessment, while the equally important considerations of esthetic value, intellectual honesty, political worth and cultural sensitivity are overlooked.

But more significant still, the deepest problem with the let's-blame-the-media school is that it ends up creating only a diversion to the central issues for serious media critics — namely, who controls and profits from the media, what is the *whole* understanding of life being purveyed, how can we challenge that understanding most effectively, by what alternative channels, and in the strength of what alternative visions?

God made it — let's use it

Far from seeing it as the devil's territory, an increasing number of Christians (especially those who have grown up with television as part of the living room furniture) see the media as a theatre for God's action in the world. They see his action incarnated in the news each night, echoed in the interplay of soap-opera romance and parabled in newspaper features that package heroism and compassion into 500-word fillers between the advertisements.

This way of seeing the media is endlessly expandable. For example, the Soviet cinema, though officially atheistic, becomes profoundly religious in the depth of its search for ultimate meaning and value. In D. H. Lawrence's phrase, "everything is something". God, it seems, has a word within every occasion that waits to be heard.

As well as the incarnated optimism of this view of media content, a variation on the same theme (though not always with quite the same theology) is applied to the mechanics of the media as well.

Why not, runs the argument, use media technology to serve the Kingdom of God? If enough clergy were trained in microphone technique along with pastoral counselling, just think of the impact the church might have. And if Christians could claim enough radio stations for evangelism in the Third World, then the Great Commission might be implemented overnight. That's overstating the case, but Raymond Davis of the Sudan Interior Mission puts it more precisely. He talks about the evangelistic power of Radio ELWA in Monrovia:

> Radio is a significant symbol of the new strategy in missions today. It is new, but not a novelty. It is glamorous, perhaps, but not a gimmick. An ideal instrument of missionary propagation in Africa, radio goes a long way in providing solutions to the fourfold problems of manpower, multiplication, mobility and maintenance.
>
> Rising from the steaming jungle, ELWA's giant steel towers symbolize the hands of men and God joined in this great venture. The incessant pounding of the nearby ocean portrays

the pulsating heart of God, as defined in the call-letter slogan Eternal Love Winning Africa.

Climbing the high walls of prejudice and opposition that isolate nations as well as individuals, ELWA speaks to the heart in the privacy of the home... (linking) the hungry hearts of Africa's great peoples, however remote, with the one who said, "I am the living bread which came down from heaven".*

---

* Foreword to Jane Reed & Jim Grant: *Voice Under Every Palm.* Grand Rapids, Mich.: Zondervan Publishing House, 1968.

The best hope for world mission in this view might well be the ever cheaper and ever more available transistor. If only we could turn up the volume high enough in enough places, the Word would be heard and the world would believe.

But it wouldn't, of course. For no matter how sophisticated the church's electronic evangelists become, God remains as mysterious and hidden as ever and the Gospel's demands just as impossible. No matter how good the reception is, the Word is never transmitted direct and the nearest we come to a live performance is when we read or see or hear second-hand how someone else experiences it first-hand.

This mediated character of faith is rarely given adequate acknowledgment by the churches' electronic enthusiasts who reduce Gospel communication to a question of technique.

The technological approach to Christian thinking about the media produces judgments that value quantity over quality. The bigger the investment — the bigger the result in the numbers you attract. It might work for selling soap but not for the Gospel, as Anglican writer and media commentator Trevor Beeson explains:

> The Christian Gospel offers liberation and the possibility of living life to the full, but it also makes considerable demands. The way to resurrection is through the cross and there are many reasons why individuals are unable to accept its demands. If the life and ministry of Jesus offers a model for the church in every age, there is every reason for supposing that the number of those who can receive the Gospel in its fullness will always be relatively small. This being so, it may well be that the more effective communication of the Gospel will lead to a diminution of the number of people who describe themselves as Christians and who are ready to identify themselves with the church. In many parts of the western world the prevailing expressions of the Christian faith represent serious distortions of the message of Jesus, and commitment to the church is based on social, psychological and conventional demands. In such a situation a clear communication of the Gospel might have a devastating effect upon the existing church communities.*

The underlying problem with so much of the God-made-it-let's-use-it approach to the media is plain naiveté. The Christian technocrats underestimate the real complexity of communicating the Gospel, while the equally gullible incarnationists go overboard, seeing God in and between every line and image with as much discrimination as a primitive worshipper of rocks and trees.

But short of surrendering the world to the devil and concentrating all energies on communication with the already saved, Christians have no choice but to stay with the incarnationist approach to the media. The real challenge is to find

---

* *An Eye for an Ear*, p. 108. London: SCM Press Ltd., 1972.

a way of trusting God's presence and action within the media without becoming a victim of the media in the process.

As a confirmed incarnationist on media matters, anxious to take advantage of whatever air or column space is offered, I vividly remember the demeaning feeling that remained after taping a series of three minute "Epilogue" television programmes that were used to mop up the dregs of a Sunday evening's viewing.

Sat firmly in a studio chair, squarely in front of the one available camera, without the budget possibility of moving anything but my hands, I played out the victim role Sunday after Sunday. Finally, in a rather desperate attempt to alter the inevitable, I made a direct plea to my viewers as they headed off to bed. "Please don't turn me off," I begged. Then, hopefully before they had a chance to recover from such a crude appeal, I launched into an irrelevant explanation of why the clerical collar I wore was actually cut from a butcher's plastic apron. The content of the whole programme amounted to little more than a song-and-dance act of holy foolishness, but looking back on it now, at least its intention was clear — to protest against the impossibly compromised and naive position I had placed myself in for the sake of "religious" broadcasting.

The format, scheduling, planning and philosophy of the whole venture was entirely set up to suit the media and the churches' best interests were dismissed with an almost contemptuous disregard. Any less suitable use of the media for the Gospel's sake was hard to imagine.

By over-rating the importance of such access to the media, failing to analyse beforehand the real implications of being used and controlled in this way, and fearing to challenge (except for that one silly protest) the shape and style of the programme, I had become a media victim.

This is clear to me now, but it wasn't then because my view of the media was one of undiscriminating gratitude for the opportunities it gave me. A critical analysis of the way it shaped the world and defined the terms on which I should enter it — that hadn't crossed my mind as a possibility, let alone a responsibility.

II. Getting to know
the monster

in which we reminisce about encyclopedia salesmen and the rising price of information, suggest some questions for the media to help call its bluff, then open up the issues of transnational ownership and control of the media, and the way information is packaged and squeezed into shape — Donald Duck's assistance is gratefully acknowledged.

I came from a home where education was held to be a Good Thing and information was seen as the way to broader minds and better lives. My parents knew that and so did the encyclopedia salesmen who were forever knocking at the front door with promises of enlightenment in ten volumes. They talked about investing in the children's future with a small deposit now to secure the whole series plus annual supplements until 1995.

What these silver-tongued gentlemen were offering was information as a highly commercial commodity. Even at the time I can remember thinking it a little strange that you had to pay so much for knowledge that everywhere else in the community was dispensed free of charge by teachers, clergy, journalists and traffic policemen. (Maybe that's why the encyclopedias were such lavishly bound volumes — you at least had the feeling you got your money's worth in paper.)

But the encyclopedia-selling of my childhood was an amateur exercise compared to the sophistication and scale of the information industry today. As a commodity sold to gain power and profit, information has become a resource like iron ore, to be dug up, processed and dispensed to the most profitable market. Except that unlike iron ore, there's an unlimited source of supply and an endless variety of ways in which it can be used and sold.

Christians concerned with understanding the impact and effect of the media have somehow to come to terms with the commercial value of information, especially if they ever hope to break down the image of the media as all-powerful, all-knowing, and with all our best interests at heart.

So strong a mystique has the media created, so sure has it become of its own importance and so confident of its way of understanding the truth, that any attempt at such critical analysis seems to be a foolish Don Quixote-style exercise from the start, certainly beyond the ability of any small church groups.

For there are few institutions left in modern society that speak with such daunting assurance about their role and expect their public to agree so readily. To illustrate this self-confidence, consider the advice given in Appendix I on how to approach the media.

This chapter is to suggest that such an exercise is not as daunting as it seems. There are resources easily available to even the smallest and most unqualified group that help people to cut the media down to size, laugh at its pretensions and thereby feel free enough to challenge and cope with its effects on our lives.

Any such media analysis proceeds best by working on two fronts at once — the very local and the very international. Without the wider context, the local analysis is illusory, for nothing your nearest newspaper, radio or television station does is free from outside conditioning — be it in the form of a balance sheet, racial and political stereotypes or the order of the items on the seven o'clock news.

In the same way, international analyses of corporate communication structures and value judgments remain abstract unless they're earthed in how the media reports, distorts, supports and profits from life in your own neighbourhood.

Locally, the best place to start is with the men and women who manage the media nearest to you — the newspapers, magazines, radio and television stations. All of them claim a public service motivation, yet rarely are they pressed to define publicly the assumptions on which their service should proceed. What's more, media people themselves are helped by being asked to say how they go about deciding what is news, what are their self-imposed limits in seeking out material, what criteria they use in selecting and rearranging that material, why some subjects are always covered and others never touched. Appendix II offers a list of useful exercises for beginning such a dialogue with your local media.

Develop an exchange around questions like these suggested and very quickly the ambiguity, uncertainty and plain confusion of much media activity becomes clear. So do the very severe limits under which the media operate: the often unconscious boundaries set by commercial sponsorship, the restraints of deadlines and available space and time that work against depth and breadth of coverage. Your media criticism will certainly become sharper and better informed as a result. It might also become more sympathetic!

Another aspect of your dialogue with local media needs to focus on ownership and control — who holds control over finance, editorial policy, information sources, hiring and firing of personnel? How much local consultation is there and what form does it take? How is public response taken into account — by what sort of survey and how frequently? Discussion about greater public participation in the media is fashionable right now — but usually with as much real involvement as laboratory mice have in the direction of modern science.

All of this local exploration needs a wider framework. For even the smallest and seemingly independent small-town newspaper is shaped by its stake in the international communications-industrial complex, rivalled in size only by its military counterpart, and "guided to a great extent by the interests of the corporate marriage between transnational industry and transnational banking".

That at least is the conclusion of Dutch communication researcher Dr Cees Hamelink whose definitive studies of the transnational communication industry, *Perspectives for Public Community* and *The Corporate Village*, leave the reader with a cold chill at the thought of such concentrated and largely uncontrolled power over information.

Transnationals control up to 75% of the flow of international communication, Dr Hamelink's studies reveal, and 60% of those corporations are US-based. In the film industry alone, American films occupy over 50% of the whole world's screen time. But the same studies uncover even more disturbing inequities. For the imbalance of influence, interest and control in the communication industry is most clearly revealed when you consider the worldwide distribution of news correspondents employed by the four giant news services that monopolize the flow of information in the West. The example of Africa says it all. Out of a total of some 1,200 full-time foreign correspondents employed by the four major wire services, there is a maximum of 70 full-time agency journalists based in Africa, covering a continent of some 350 million people — 10% of the world's population. And elsewhere in the Two-Thirds World, this distribution is concentrated in those centres of greatest economic interest for the West.

That's hardly surprising when you consider that Associated Press and United Press International, for instance, draw 80% of their overall revenue from their domestic market. For all their talk of worldwide coverage, the news sources on which your local media rely are heavily shaped by what the folks back home want to hear and are willing to pay for the privilege. Despite all the technological breakthroughs in the communication industry and after all the claims of greater international sharing and understanding, the global information flow (secular or religious) still runs from North to South and West to East almost as strongly as it did in the days when superior Northerners and Westerners still believed that was the way it ought to be.

This chapter doesn't pretend to compete with the exhaustive analysis of other books on just how deeply the communication industry is ensnared in the economic structures and value framework of transnational corporations and their reliance on ever-greater growth. In western developed nations where production capacity already exceeds consumer demand, new appetites and markets for communication sales have to be constantly cultivated. And the greenest fields are usually in the Two-Thirds World where commercial sponsorship is already established as the norm for the development of broadcasting services.

The hope that developing nations might be able to free information from its commercial captivity seems to grow more remote as their media systems expand. And where commercial captivity of the media isn't a threat, political captivity certainly is. Nobody, nowhere, lets information go free, any more than gold or uranium is given away. But our attempt to look the media monster in the eye must go beyond asking who holds the power and also consider how that power is employed. Here the analysis needed becomes more complex than ever.

For if an accountant's bionic eye for balance sheets is needed to sort out the economic intricacies of transnational ownership and influence, then a poet's feel for subtlety and implication is needed to see the way the media manages and packages its material.

The weapons in this section of the media armoury are multitudinous: omission, innuendo, over and under dimensioning, stereotype and shift of context are all used, often unconciously by well-meaning commentators who have never got around to recognizing their own cultural, racial and political blinkers.

Crime reports in the New Zealand press, to take one small example, used to regularly inform readers whether or not a defendant was a Maori or a Polynesian. But if the person in question was European, that fact was considered not worth mentioning.

In the western press more generally, the same sort of selective coverage is evident when we're reminded that a person is a communist (but not a capitalist), or an attractive women (but rarely an attractive man).

Constantly, and with great subtlety, the media through the choice and style of its presentation (to say nothing of the accompanying barrage of advertisements) is telling us what is normal, proper, healthy, sexy and satisfying. And cleverly mixed in with that advice, the values of private ownership, greater efficiency, and more rapid growth are being exhorted all the time. What's good and fine and worthy is continually being preselected by an all-wise media that knows better than we do what are the "*Top* Stories of the Week" and the "*Highlights* of the Half-Hour". Everything from the "*best*" of Beethoven to the "*real* inside story" on the Middle East is chosen and laid out for us with incredible presumption.

One of the most amusing yet revealing examples of how the media structures the way we're meant to see the world is given by Ariel Dorfman and Armand Mattelart in their study on *How to Read Donald Duck*:

The realm of Disney is not one of fantasy, for it does react to world events. Its vision of Tibet is not identical to its vision of Indochina. Fifteen years ago the Caribbean was a sea of pirates. Disney has had to adjust to the fact of Cuba and the invasion of the Dominican Republic. The buccaneer now cries "Viva the Revolution", and has to be defeated. It will be Chile's turn yet.

Searching for a jade elephant, Scrooge and his family arrive in Unsteadystan, "where every thug wants to be ruler", and "where there is always someone shooting at someone else".

A state of civil war is immediately turned into an incomprehensible game of someone-or-other against any ethical direction or socio-economic *raison d'être*. The war in Vietnam becomes a mere interchange of unconnected and senseless bullets, and a truce becomes a siesta.

"Wahn Beeg Rhat, yes Duckburg, no!" cries a guerilla in support of an ambitious (communist) dictator, as he dynamites the Duckburg embassy. Noticing that his watch is not working properly, the Vietcong (no less) mutters: "Shows you can't trust these watches from the 'worker's paradise'." The struggle for power is purely personal, the eccentricity of ambition: "Hail to Wahn Beeg Rhat, dictator of all the happy people", goes the cry and sotto voce, "Happy or not". Defending his conquest, the dictator gives orders to kill. "Shoot him, don't let him spoil my revolution." The saviour in this chaotic situation is Prince Char Ming, also known (in the Spanish version) as Yho Soy ("I am" — the English is Soy Bheen), names expressive of his magical egocentricity. He comes to reunify the country and "pacify" the people. He is destined to triumph, because the soldiers refuse to obey the orders of a leader who has lost his charisma, who is not "Char Ming". So one guerilla wonders why they "keep these silly revolutions going forever". Another denounces them, demanding a return to the King, "like in the good old days".*

So much for the neutral innocence of mass media for children. Even in its elementary and entertaining aspect there's more going on than meets the eye or the ear. No wonder that the Senegalese director general of Unesco, Amadou Mahtar M'Bow, accuses the western media of "systematically stressing the phenomena of tensions or violence in the countries of the Third World" so that people in those nations "see their faces reflected from afar in mirrors that deform them".

That deformation has become so widespread that viewers, listeners and readers of the First and Second World as well as the Third come to take the distortions for granted. Every African with a gun must be a terrorist, every woman dressed in less than a neck-to-knee costume is automatically awaiting seduction, every old person is by definition only capable of kindness to children and reminiscing about the good old days.

But picking random examples of how thoroughly the media has stage-managed our view of the world is finally a futile exercise. Instead of complaining about what we've got, the real task is to suggest an outline of the kind of media we want, then set about challenging the existing structures as discerning consumers or contributors.

---

* I. G. Editions, Inc., 1975, quoted in Cees Hamelink: *The Corporate Village*, p. 151. Rome: IDOC International, 1977.

III. Gospel marks
for the media

in which the scene is set for applying Gospel insights to media evaluation, and the search for a distinctly "Christian media" is seen as a dead-end street, along with the search for Christian asparagus-growing.

When Christians try to focus their faith on any aspect of life, the danger arises of using the Gospel as a double standard: applying it very generally but not too rigorously to the secular world (be good, be kind, don't swear), then saving the really serious application for the church and other explicitly religious activities. The implication is that the Gospel has more to say to the saved inside the sanctuary than it does to the unwashed outside.

This double-standard habit is especially evident in discussions about all sorts of Christian specialities — from architecture to economics, embroidery to organ music. A special Christian version of these disciplines is often assumed, though nobody in their right mind ever talks about Christian truck-driving or asparagus-growing, or even Christian carpentry, despite the biblical mandate that trade could claim. The only theological sense to be made of such activities is to say that Christians engage in them and make their witness by the skill and care and purpose they display in the process.

So too with Christian media. As a category it is meaningless, for the churches' communication enterprises are as corrupt and compromised as anyone else's, perhaps not motivated so often by the profit motive but just as entangled with ambition for power and prestige and self-interest, institutional or personal. For the church to defend its media as a special case, governed by different rules than those which apply to other communicators who also seek to reflect the true shape of the world around them, is to end up with a church press that fails to fulfil the most basic standards of clarity, honesty, accuracy, openness and effective outreach.

Nor is it acceptable to claim that even though the Christian media mightn't always perform any better than its secular counterpart, its ideals and intentions are higher. Consider the following statement of media purpose:

"To be invariably on the side of patriotism, legality, courage... to expose injustices, to right wrongs, to give advice, to befriend the friendless and help the helpless."

The highest-minded Christian paper would be hard pressed to outdo that credo. In actual fact, it was written in 1955 by Britain's National Press Council as a description of the task attempted by that country's popular press — the same press that others have described as exploitative, reactionary, mercenary, crude and consistently destructive of human value and dignity.

Whether we measure the media by what it claims to achieve or actually does, the case for talking about a distinctive "Christian media" becomes a tail-chasing exercise. We get further by seeing media communication as a common function, put to a whole variety of purposes — everything from sharing the faith to telling the news to selling sausage meat.

But however it's done and for whatever purpose, the Gospel has something to say about the media's performance and task. I believe the guidelines that follow are consistent with that Gospel. Other people might arrive at the same conclusions from other faith assumptions, for clearly Christians are not the only believers whose faith compels them to condemn the exploitative, dishonest and subhuman features of the mass media.

But these conclusions I arrived at as a Christian working for the media. I share them in the spirit that I found them — as part of a journey that God has made ahead of us, into the heart of his world, where he waits for us to meet him. And the sign of his presence there might well be contained in the next television commercial or buried at the bottom of a back-page story.

POUR VOUS
YOU
POUR TOI
PERSONALIZE
WE AT TRANS-N LOVE YOU
FREE
KRISPY KRUNCHY
MADE JUST FOR YOU
YCS

IV. A Gospel
way of relating

in which the great media fraud of making personal promises then failing to deliver is attacked; the Gospel's plea for keeping things personal is elaborated; some ways of building and measuring personal quality are suggested; we speculate on why the media finds it so hard to say it's sorry, and why media consumers must be able to answer back.

Have you ever had the experience of flying with an airline after reading its advertisements about the wonderfully personal service it provides? The colour photos and the clever copy-writing have led you to expect that the stewardess's smile will be meant just for you and the menu, even though it mightn't actually offer a choice, will be prepared with precisely your tastes in mind. Appetite whetted, you board the plane to find it's overcrowded and your seat is double-booked. The flustered stewardess's smile slowly turns into a snarl and when you're finally seated (next to an over-sized neighbour who has already claimed your elbow room), a plastic portioned meal is served with a flavour that makes you keep checking whether you aren't actually chewing the paper napkins.

It's all part of the media's greatest hoax — the promise of something personal from an utterly impersonal industry. And the bigger and more mechanized it grows, through merger, take-over and new technology, the more strident that promise of a personal touch becomes.

The media can't claim that contradiction for itself alone, of course. It permeates every corner of industrial urban society. Wherever things get bigger for efficiency's sake, the mythology of personal interest is cultivated with greater fervour. So we have huge supermarkets claiming to have the individual human character of the street-corner grocers they swallowed out of business long ago. Giant insurance conglomerates claiming that every policy-holder is a genuine friend. Drug companies claiming personal concern about everything from the regularity of your bowels to the softness of your skin.

The media builds this double-think mentality, nursing our collective illusion of a society that really can be more warm and intimate even as people grow colder and more separate from each other; simpler and manageable, even as transnational economic forces make it more complex and further beyond our control. But we keep listening to the false personal promises because we really do want to believe them. Like the baked-bean manufacturer who has his personal signature as a guarantee of quality on every label. We see it and accept it, while knowing deep down that the promise counts for nothing more than a can of beans.

The mass media is as guilty of this personalized deception as the rest of society, not only by spreading the hoax through its public relations and advertising services, but also in terms of its own self-image.

For there is no picture of itself that the media favours more than the one in which it stands as valiant champion of individual rights and freedoms, comforting the lonely with the company of its electronic image, reassuring the troubled with the star-struck promise of its horoscopes and the advertised remedies for acne and heartache, thundering out self-righteous editorial indignation against the evils of permissiveness, while leering over them in careful detail.

"Subscribe, tune in, turn on to us and we'll make you one of the family," is the media's most common promotional theme song. A community you can enter with the flick of a page or switch, painlessly, instantly joined, but utterly incapable of offering any warmth or redemption at all.

The first and clearest call of the Christian Gospel to the media is for an end to this sham by demanding that promises personally made are personally delivered, and when they're not, exposing the pretence and laughing it into embarrassed withdrawal.

Because Christians, of all people, have a vested interest in keeping things personal and protecting the authentic character of every human encounter. Every Gospel response to the events of the day relies on earthing what's happening around us in questions of personal responsibility and meaning and dignity.

That is the method Jesus developed. He dealt with people by looking them in the eye. He answered the great theological issues of his day by anchoring them to stories of personal accountability. Whenever there was a crisis to be faced, a lesson to be learnt, a job to be done, Jesus made it personal, whether it was a matter of identifying a neighbour, feeding a crowd or answering a charge of treason.

Nowhere is there any room in the Christian understanding of life for treating each other as objects to be used. The only truly human status is that of subject — as people who have to be accepted and respected, even as we try to influence and persuade them.

No matter how noble the purpose of the exercise, whether it's to sell Jesus or chewing gum, that subject-object distinction remains crucial to the Gospel understanding of media integrity. There is no way in which we can help people become more human by treating them as less than human in the process. By abusing people's privacy, exploiting their sexuality, stereotyping their race and culture, caricaturing their beliefs and insulting their intelligence, journalists destroy the human element in their human interest stories. Warm-blooded subjects become cold cardboard objects, often in exactly those publications and programmes that promise the most intimate and private revelations.

One very clear barometer for testing the truly personal quality in any communication process is the tone that the media conveys and the style it adopts. For the tone of a message reveals the attitude taken towards the receiver, and the style reveals the way in which the writer or speaker takes him or herself.

So over-simplicity is read as lack of respect for the receiver's intelligence; over-enthusiasm is seen as a sign of dishonesty; cliched phrases as a mark of a dull mind; too many qualifications reveal timidity; too fussily personal a tone is taken as a hint of egoism and self-importance; too general and abstract a tone is heard as evasiveness or ignorance of the full story.

Whether the media intends it or not, viewers, listeners, and readers personally interpret the messages they receive.

The Gospel message helps us say thank God for that and let's try and keep it that way.

The old-fashioned evangelist's embarrassing insistence on always keeping the conversation personal with a call for a decision at the end is exactly what we need to rediscover in our media analysis. By demanding journalists to explain why they write what they do, editors to justify how they select material, programmers to share the reasons for their choices, we are meeting the media in a way that the Gospel says we should — as a personal affair.

But to turn criticism personal is to play dirty in our society. That's because our personal dealings with each other are too often handled in a fragmented, isolated way, outside the framework and discipline that interpersonal *relationships* require. The editor of my local paper writes what I consider to be the most reactionary and racist accounts of what's happening in Rhodesia. I've also heard that his opinions are heavily influenced by the fact that his co-pilot in the air force during World War II was a white Rhodesian farmer. But I've never got round to meeting the editor and asking him if that's true, inviting him to speak or complimenting him on his coverage of the controversy over local school facilities last year.

Without the context of a relationship, then, all my efforts to analyse the media and encourage personal honesty are hollow noises. They allow no room for *response*, which is the hallmark of quality in any dialogue between the giver and receiver of information.

But to invite response is a risky business. It might mean that deeply-felt beliefs are upset. It will certainly open up unwelcome complexity that the mass media seems structurally incapable of handling.

For there is no single more difficult thing for the media to do than apologize openly for passing on information that is incorrect or incomplete. A 1977 Liberation News Service cartoonist pictures the height of media absurdity by drawing a square-eyed viewer in front of his television set, listening to the bland little announcer begin his bulletin: "And now the news at eleven. To begin with, everything I said on the six o'clock news was wrong."

Anyone who has ever tried to get a correction published or a wrong impression corrected in the media won't find anything outlandish about that cartoon.

The difficulty in getting the media to make room for critical responses from readers, listeners or viewers reveals just how one-sided the relationship really is. To confess anything less than complete wisdom is to threaten the objectivity and confidence that is so much part of the media's self-understanding. But saying that won't change anything — the creative and open climate that two-way relationships can encourage has to be demonstrated by those parts of the media with the courage to try.

And it's here that church-sponsored communicators have a special opportunity. For what other body than the church has a clearer mandate to see communication as incomplete without an answer from the people being addressed? For the Gospel understands God as one who makes himself vulnerable to our refusal of him, who gives his people the freedom to say yes or no.

So when the media dares to invite and allow the fullest possible public participation in shaping the content of its communication, it is not only demonstrating the quality of a relationship. An insight about the nature of God himself is also being reflected.

A great mid-west American preacher used to tell his congregation the story of Job in all its baffling injustice. Finally, having established the divine mystery that the story reveals, he would end by asking: "And what sort of a way is that to run a world?", then step down from the pulpit. The sermon was finished but the exposition of the text would continue until the congregation had finished making their response. Communication was reliant on a relationship in which giver and receiver changed places again and again. It's a model that most of the media has yet to discover or trust.

But there are exceptions. Take the theologically evangelical, politically radical *Sojourners* magazine in Washington, DC, which is thoroughly committed to this writing-out-of-a-relationship approach. "We want to get more of ourselves into an encounter with the things that are," says *Sojourners* editor Jim Wallis. "We try to be present ourselves, as reporters and disciples, in the midst of our stories."

Wallis gives the example of a *Sojourners* journalist assigned to cover a huge evangelical media conference. The event was a mix of right-wing politics, big money and celebrity Christians, all of which the *Sojourners* man found repulsive. But he persisted in establishing relationships with as many of the conference people as he could reach and wrote his final story about the surprisingly wide personal experience of human encounter that resulted. The conference was covered, not with any pretence of objectivity, but certainly with a depth and integrity that could be seen and respected by all who attended.

Without that willingness to write from within a relationship, Wallis believes the "article would either have been a public relations piece for the convention or just a hatchet job by somebody with our point of view".

The immediate criticism that this approach to communication evokes is that it's not "objective" enough. That's a problem we'll confront directly in the next chapter but the people at *Sojourners* aren't daunted at all by the accusation:

The "objective" approach is impossible for us because we don't see ourselves just as detached observers. We can't assume a totally detached relationship from those people we are talking to and writing about even when we feel, and many times with good reason, that they're our adversaries. What we've said about letting ourselves come through in the stories also applies to the way in which we do the stories as well.

So, if we are going to do something critical, as we have about right-wing Christian political action and evangelism, or something about Billy Graham finances or whatever, in all those cases we have to take into account the relationship that we have with those people and the way we've come to work it out. That is to say, our intention has to be that of building the body of Christ. It's a discerning, revealing, proving intention but beneath it all, our action is motivated by a deep concern for the integrity and the life, validity, the health of the body of Christ. This applies particularly when we're doing journalism about the church, about the religious kind of community. Now, we think that the way in which that life is best built up is by dealing with the truth of what is going on, not by hiding it behind something, like keeping relationships in order, for example. We think that honest relationships can only get established when we really are being truthful. But it makes it a much more difficult process for us personally, so I think it's important to say that our not being detached cuts both ways. It not only has something to say about the perspective with which we approach our goals. It also has something to say about the way we go about writing.

As the *Sojourners* experience suggests, this personally engaged, relationship-based style of communication is enormously demanding on its practitioners. The mass media find it much easier to retreat behind the defence of objectivity and the claim to be above personal interest or institutional bias.

Journalists who work without that impossible pretence are much more vulnerable, but they are probably much closer to the Gospel stance. For the truth of what they write depends on the depth of their engagement rather than the height of their detachment. And the Gospel, biased as it is in favour of the oppressed and the poor, harbours no illusions about the option of neutrality. By refusing to choose, you in fact do make a choice, in favour of the status quo. And there's nothing objective about that.

V. A Gospel way of seeing

in which we get it all together with a word or two on inter-relatedness and wholeness, then argue that the biggest obstacle to Christian communication is not the media, but the church and its one-eyed way of looking at the world.

In our search for Gospel marks that might be applied to any analysis of the media, we've talked in terms of how issues should be treated, always personally and always in the context of a relationship. But the Gospel also has something to say about how issues should be seen. This chapter attempts to trace how the Gospel's way of seeing can be used as a measure of media performance.

The word that says it all — inter-relatedness — has become a truism in ecumenical social thought, but it remains as elusive as ever to communicate, especially when it comes to applying it to any assessment of the media. How can the connection between the local and the global and the multi-dimensional nature of modern life be represented in a 30-second news bulletin, a two-column story or a single photograph?

Efforts are already underway to communicate the inter-relatedness of life in the global village. The more adventurous corners of the mass media use guest commentators with opposing views to the established editorial line. A few take advantage of alternative news, information and research services such as International Documentation and Communication Centre (IDOC) in Rome, Counter Information Service in London, the Canadian Information Sharing System, New Asia News in Tokyo, or Latin America Press in Lima, Peru.

In these ways, new perspectives are brought to old political understandings and there is a growing attempt to cover issues with a multi-disciplinary approach. We're slowly recognizing that psychologists might have something to say about Christmas, as well as theologians, and theologians in turn may have their own perspectives to offer on the next parliamentary election that won't fit at all with the all-embracing punditry of the political scientists.

In the field of development education, a new breed of resource people known as *animateurs* help the public see new

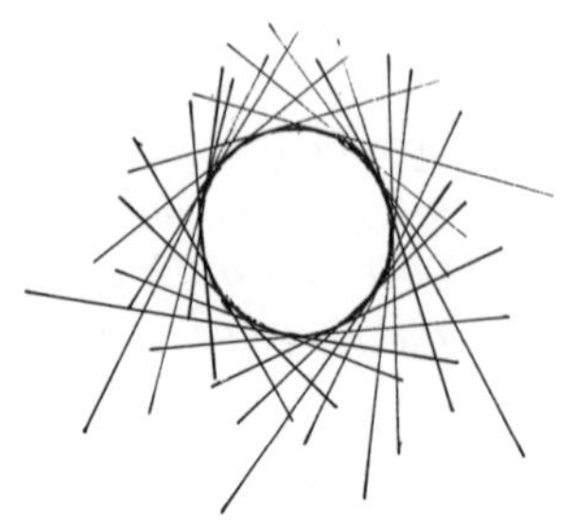

connections between third-world poverty and first-world life-style, home-town politics and international trading. They focus on single commodities such as tea, dried milk or agricultural seeds, then trace the local and global implications involved in the production, distribution and control of each item.

Such efforts make it impossible to avoid seeing the global way in which our poverty and affluence (materially and spiritually) intertwine, and the pressure on the media to communicate this interdependence increases accordingly.

The churches' best contribution to this pressure might well be to deal more convincingly with inter-relatedness in her own ranks before giving advice on the subject to others. For as Christians we've long been guilty of an if-it's-not-religious-it's-not-relevant approach. And if that seems to be an overstatement, count up the column inches of the local church press that don't have an ecclesiastical angle, then ask yourself whether there's not some truth in the charge of religious myopia. With a few brave exceptions, there's still little evidence in most church papers that God might ever work outside the church or that his presence is ever felt without the approval and prior arrangement of a synod or church council.

But the issue is not simply one of opening up the columns of the local church press or filling the air time available to the churches with material that goes beyond the public relations interests of the sponsors.

To do justice to the wholeness of the Gospel in the media also requires that we see the way we communicate in its wholeness as well. For our most powerful statements about the faith are usually not the self-conscious attempts we make through the mass media at all. We speak more clearly through the style of our church buildings and the uses we put them to, in the way we invest our money, the modesty of our life-style, our choice of careers and clothing, our presence among the people who hurt most and whose voices are least able to be heard.

I once served on the staff of a parish church that was used by a small congregation for traditional worship on Sunday, by solo parents for dancing and socializing on Wednesday, and a homosexual group for study, discussion and prayer on Thursday. The communication power of simply making the building available in this way was enormous. We could have had an hour a night on television to tell the city that the Gospel's good news about acceptance was meant for everyone. But it would not have had the same effect.

"The primary means of Christian communication", says Trevor Beeson, experienced though he is in the power of the mass media, "is the church itself."

The Christian faith has never been effectively communicated by a corrupt church. There have been periods in history when the church has produced monumental buildings and theologies. There have been times when the church has exercised extensive temporal power and taken possession of the consciences of individuals. But, on the whole, these have not been eras of effective Christian communication. It is when the love of God has been revealed in the lives of individual men and women, and in the life of the church itself, that the world has been moved to enquire whether the Christian Gospel might have light to throw upon the human condition.

The same is true today. In the final resort men and women will be attracted to a place within range of the Christian gospel, not by means of the techniques of persuasion but by the quality of life they see exhibited by those who claim to be under the influence of the divine love. Pronouncements, public relations exercises, sophisticated broadcasting techniques and so forth will serve little purpose unless the life of the Christian community is a living and dynamic expression of love. The only effective visual aid and channel of Christian communication is the life of the local church.*

John Taylor, visual arts director for the World Council of Churches, has made a terrifying film about the church's success in communicating itself and thereby the Gospel. A brief minute or two long, the film depicts a television viewer

---

* *An Eye for an Ear*, p. 112. London: SCM Press Ltd., 1972.

sunk in an armchair and drinking beer as he watches a preacher at work on the small screen. The sermon finally finishes, the viewer burps loudly and the film ends.

Such a view is probably as realistic as it is dismal an assessment. But if it helps us take our failure seriously, that will be progress indeed. Not as a failure in the charisma or lack of it exhibited by television preachers, but rather as a failure to realize the communication power inherent in the life of the whole church. To see that communication potential in its full breadth will be to ensure that we share our faith more effectively and assess the role of the mass media more realistically.

VI. A Gospel way of measuring

in which the impossible Gospel scale of possibility is described, the odds against success are rated as ridiculous and we explain how that isn't a cause for concern. Some ecumenical experiments are printed with pride and the power of parables is celebrated as something thankfully beyond our understanding. Airline theology is grounded and a walk in the dark is recommended.

The World Council of Churches' staff member in charge of the programme to uncover and fight the abuses of transnational corporations has decorated his Geneva office wall with drawings from a children's fairy tale. They're taken from *Gulliver's Travels* and depict the giant Gulliver pinned to the ground by a mass of Lilliputian threads.

A Taiwanese theologian and WCC staff member, asked to write in a serious academic quarterly about the understanding of mission inherent in the plans for a world conference on evangelism, spends half his article recounting the story of *Alice in Wonderland* and unravelling Alice's allegorical meeting with the mouse in the pool of tears.

And an article in *One World* magazine on the WCC's ambitious programme thrust "Towards a Just, Participatory and Sustainable Society" begins by stammering over the title, "The Just and... er... P... P..." and fooling around with its various abbreviations. The same magazine, in a subsequent issue, argues that an appropriate symbol for the worldwide ecumenical movement is the circus clown — outlandishly dressed, attempting the ridiculous for the sake of its audience.

All these examples express a common theme of impossibility. They speak of the fact that the church's mission and the Gospel's demands are hopelessly out of scale with anything we can ever hope to achieve, let alone even fully understand.

Whether our task is media analysis or evangelism, the odds are against success before we start. For the resources recommended by the Gospel for our struggle are not billion dollar campaign chests, organizational development charts or armies of experts, but the shield of faith, the breastplate of righteousness, and the whole armour of love.

Stated like that, the advice seems like pious claptrap. And it is if you use the protection of love's armour as an excuse for not ever translating that love into hard questions and real actions that might well require money and planning, and even an expert or two.

But the point of contrasting the itemized language of warehouse inventory with the abstract language of faith is to help us get our perspective clear before we start. The church's role is not to take over the world (God has already made a successful bid for that) but to act as a sign in and for the world of what it means in Christ to be fully human.

The signs that the Gospel suggests we trust are invariably fragmented, tiny and if not inappropriate then certainly incomplete. A candle in the darkness, a mustard seed in the forest, five loaves and two fishes to cater for a hungry crowd of thousands, a carpenter's son for a messiah to save the world and, for the grand climax, a crucifixion.

When it comes to media analysis and action by the churches, the same impossible Gospel scale of possibility holds true. Our task is not to take over NBC, reform the editorial policies of *The Daily Telegraph* or start a broadcasting network that will drown out atheistic programmes.

The job is rather, in a hundred different tiny ways and places, to expose where the media is unjust, inhuman and full of deceit; to support where it is creative, caring and seeking out the truth; and most important of all, to demonstrate through the church's own communication structures and strategies, a better way of speaking out and listening in.

It's that demonstration of what we want the media to be that matters most of all. And as members of a worldwide ecumenical fellowship, there are already examples we can hold up with pride:

• The Caribbean Conference of Churches newspaper *Contact*, which serves as the only regional forum for that much exploited island territory divided against itself by a colonial past.

• The Netherlands-based *Interfilm* organization, an international interchurch network that offers an alternative system of film distribution and a unique dialogue with the commercial cinema world through special juries at film festivals, research, conferences, etc.

• The *Sojourners* community mentioned earlier which offers a magazine of radical biblical reflection as one of its several ministries to the oppressed people of Washington and the captivity of the church in American society.

• The Kenyan churches weekly *Target* with its outspoken tradition of Gospel engagement in the turmoil of East African political and social change.

• The New Zealand Methodists' newspaper *New Citizen* which for ten years has been pioneering ecumenical journalism in defiance of economic hardship and denominational indifference.

None of these examples can pretend to compete with the power and resources of the transnationally-owned mass media. The production costs of one single issue of *Time* magazine would exceed the annual working budgets of the whole list. There are a hundred other such examples of equal courage and creativity (many of them supported by the World Association for Christian Communication), all of them with a power that *Time* can never hope to claim.

It's what the Gospel calls the power of the parable. Jesus relied on it and became the most powerful story-teller of all time as a result.

Parable actions have some distinguishing marks. The first is the ring of shared experience. Parables are heard because they contain glimpses of pain and doubt and joy that resonate in the receivers' own lives. It is precisely through the difficulties and inadequacies (understaffing, underfinancing, inexperience, inadequate equipment) of all these examples I've listed that they are able to speak so strongly. Anyone who has ever tried anything impossible identifies with them immediately.

The theology that undergirds these parable enterprises is not the airline-seat variety that reads as though it is written from 30,000 feet above the earth. Parable theology is incarnated theology, well-grounded in the sweat and smell of the ordinary.

For the stuff of parables is simple, everyday stuff. Ordinary enough to explain a universe and summarize a mystery; to find lost coins and wayward sons, build families and communities, win justice for a neighbour, offer love, enable healing, watch death, await a resurrection.

Somehow, in the very ordinariness of these stories, something eternal is embedded. In the truth about the least things we glimpse the truth about the greatest.

But even more distinctive is the dynamic that gives these parables their power, and thereby tells us how we can be heard. For it isn't a dynamic that depends on size, experience, strength or reputation. But rather the same dynamic that lies behind setting a light on a hill or planting leaven in a lump of dough.

The New Testament tells us that we're known by our fruits but never insists on measuring the crop by its size or cash value. The economy of grace works within a much wider framework that can't be contained in annual reports, readership surveys and quarterly feasibility studies.

New hope, dignity restored, meaning discovered... experienced today or held in promise for a later generation. These are the differences that parables make. And that's why they're finally unmeasurable differences. If we dare to attempt such changes, we can't hope to start indexing the results immediately.

Anyway, the New Testament cautions us about measuring results. It tells us not to spend too long in weighing what might happen. For our motivation depends on our openness to the prompting of the Spirit, and not on the promise of impressive results. And if what we attempt is an expression of that Spirit, it will make its mark regardless, whatever the odds against.

"For nothing is hid that shall not be made manifest, nor anything secret that shall not be known and come to light." (Luke 8 : 17).

That, of course, makes it hard to assess the real effects of our communication parables, whether they take the form of analysing other media systems or building models of our own. For a while we may have to walk in the dark, without the security of knowing that we're making any difference at all and certainly without the world-winning, world-changing rhetoric that blights so much Christian communication debate.

But if the dynamic of the parable is the dynamic of the light that shines through a vastly greater darkness, then we must select the tiny areas we want to start illuminating and trust the power of the one who makes the brightness possible to let it touch where he chooses.

Parable power, for that reason, is literally a power that is beyond us. And precisely because of that, we can trust it as a rationale for our impossible communications task.

VII. The great objectivity debate

in which some heretical thoughts are shared on the orthodox creed of objectivity; "new" journalism is seen as honourably old fashioned; we trace the curves of straight reporting and suggest a way around the obstacles of objectivity that the church can help to chart.

Much of the argument in this book to date could be dismissed by mass media professionals as Sunday morning sermonizing that evaporates on contact with Monday morning deadlines and news-room realities. But press the call, nevertheless, for a more personal, relationship-centred, response-inviting media and you find yourself in the middle of a huge fight with media managers, both secular and religious.

For the implications of much that we've covered so far create a clear challenge to objectivity — still the central canon of western media orthodoxy. Journalism that becomes too personal in its approach, according to this canon, is subjective and therefore unreliable. Journalism that confesses its commitment is compromised as a result. Journalism with beliefs is biased.

To challenge this orthodoxy is heretical, and writers who try often find themselves shunted off into the sidings of the media's career junctions.

The more fortunate ones end up with one of several labels used to identify deviancy from the norm. "Advocacy journalists" they're called, or "committed" or "engaged" or just plain "propagandist" or "egocentric". The choice of label depends on whether the editors in control are fundamentalist believers in the creed of objectivity, or more liberal followers of the faith. Either way the deviant is labelled, however politely, as an oddball. The friendliest and perhaps most revealing of all labels is that of "new journalism" — made famous by the highly personalized and impressionistic writing of American writer Tom Wolfe.

The label "new" is revealing because it implies that to show where you stand, how you feel and what you believe as a journalist is something that didn't used to happen in the "old" media.

The argument of this book is that the mass media has always practised "new journalism" in that sense, without ever being quite so open about it before. For the media has always interpreted the information it shares according to the context it operates from. No matter how "straight" its coverage, there are always curves created by the political and cultural setting and the experience and convictions that media staff bring with them. The contour of these curves is almost impossible to see without the help of outside observers who come from a different setting. So don't ask an Englishman to show us how subjective!y the BBC selects the news, and don't ask an Italian Roman Catholic at the Vatican to measure the detachment of *L'Osservatore Romano*.

The curves of supposedly straight reporting don't only show up in the print and broadcasting media. In the world of photography and visual arts the objectivity debate builds up with equal intensity. Photographs, it seems, for all their supposed ability to represent reality directly, can also lie, distort and express dependency and domination. To uncover how this can happen, consider the questions in Appendix III, prepared by the World Council of Churches photo section in Geneva.

The defenders of objectivity in whatever media reply by saying that nobody's perfect and that any other creed is even more open to abuse by ideologues and any old self-interest merchant armed with a typewriter or a camera.

It's true that much of the "new" or "advocacy" journalism school grew out of such bitterly dividing issues as the Vietnam war when young activist writers like Raymond Mungo used their craft deliberately to build the anti-war movement. Mungo himself attacked the hypocrisy of the media that recited battlefield body counts as though they made sense by themselves. The figures, it turned out later, were usually wrong anyway, but Mungo was trying to challenge the belief that "420 Vietcong were killed today" was by itself an objective and honest statement.

It was from the heat of that sort of experience that modern advocacy journalism grew. The real history goes much

further back, of course — to the acid inked pamphleteers and polemicists of every literary tradition, the balladeers and satirists, the folk artists and clowns who used their crafts in unashamedly subjective ways to support, ridicule and interpret the issues of the day.

This long tradition of media advocacy has certainly been often misused. But equally so has the more recent fashion of objectivity. Without the honesty of the advocates who display their assumptions openly, the "objective" media pass off one-eyed versions as the wide-eyed truth, often without acknowledging the people who constructed them.

Consider the example in Appendix IV in which a well-meaning and very committed young journalist used the statements of two widely respected marriage counsellors to fit his own conservative Christian reality, all in the name of objective reporting.

The journalistic sleight of hand that this example illustrates has been developed by the "objective" media into a highly skilled art, more often reliant on careful selectivity than downright misreporting. By leaving out significant detail, and rearranging material, the required impression can be created without a word of a lie or direct editorial comment. Consider the example of a *Time* magazine report on the World Council of Churches' grant of $ 85,000 to the Patriotic Front of Zimbabwe from the Special Fund of the Programme to Combat Racism.

WCC general secretary Philip Potter is pictured in the centre of the story, above a caption which reads: "We can't help it if missionaries get killed." The caption, a reference to the murder of white missionaries in Rhodesia, turned out to have actually come from a statement by an unnamed guerrilla leader, quoted in the story. Dr Potter, the story later revealed, had refused to make any comment on Rhodesia at all. Truth, in such media circles, is like a child's construction game, an endlessly rearrangeable kitset that you fit together to suit your editorial commitments.

It's possible to single out such instances of abuse in the name of objectivity, but any head-on critique of the objectivity creed becomes a counter-productive exercise, however carefully you frame it. So long as the "objective" position is recognized as the orthodox one, any alternative is by definition less objective and thereby less reliable. The objectivists, in western European cultures at least, have a monopoly on the best words in the vocabulary of the debate. If I have problems with the claim of objectivity, I must therefore be "subjective" and "partial". To attack the objectivists' claim of "neutrality" must mean I'm "committed", and that begins the question whispered behind-the-hand, "committed to what?"

If I challenge the "disinterested" claims of the media and urge that we find another model, the suspicions begin that I'm not a true journalist but a proclaimer, a preacher, or worse still, a propagandist. In this way the conceptual framework of objectivity locks us into a defensive posture and a one-down position before we even begin our analysis of the media.

So we need another starting point if our media critique is going to be creative in most western contexts. Second and

Third Worlders are better placed for they can appeal, as they have done effectively in Unesco debates, to the experience of their own countries where "objectivity" in post-revolutionary contexts has become a discredited ideology.

To ensure that creativity, some of the most imaginative and capable media people suggest that we treat objectivity not as creed but intention — a general direction to be followed. Not slavishly so, but rather like the Gospel treats the sabbath — as something made for people and not vice versa. After all, says this argument, the objectivity ideal, and it is only an ideal, contains many indisputably good aims — fairness, honesty, accuracy, even-handedness, and certainly the concept of wholeness so fervently defended earlier in this book.

The argument is an appealing one but there are other conceptual frameworks that make equal provision for these qualities. We needn't only defend objectivity to protect such "journalistic virtues" as honesty and fairness — both of which depend in the first place on a value commitment that true believer "objectivists" claim they don't have anyway! And even if objectivity is used by the media as intention rather than dogma, its conceptual weaknesses remain.

Biblically, it's still bad news because it makes no room for seeing the world from a position of commitment. Truth, says Jesus, is found through the eyes of faith. If you're not for it, then you're against it and the impossible neutrality in between creates not vision but fog.

Scientifically, objectivity is in equal trouble. Increasingly in the physical sciences, thanks to Dr Einstein's understanding of relativity, the old certainties about the behaviour of the universe are increasingly replaced by degrees of probability.

In the social sciences, objectivity has never made much sense, for everything from the collection of data to the way conclusions are drawn is a process of estimate and careful generality.

Through the study of linguistics, of special though still largely neglected interest to the mass media, objectivity has run into even greater difficulties. We see now more clearly than ever before how our use of language depends on our cultural, sexual, racial and political conditioning. In the history of words there are no black and whites any more. Language is a loaded weapon, able to offend, imply and alter the truth. It's a gun that goes off, whoever pulls the trigger, and for the "objective" journalist to say, "I didn't mean to point it at anyone" is no defence.

Philosophically, the objectivity ideal is locked into a western liberal tradition that renders it suspect in an international and ecumenical world. The mass media with its claim of worldwide service simply cannot afford to rely on a conceptual framework that depends so exclusively on one narrow tradition.

Through the ecumenical movement, the church has been helped to rediscover the variety of modes by which the Gospel is perceived and proclaimed — western liberal, and fundamentalist too, Latin American liberation, Asian suffering, East European mystical, the list of alternatives goes on. The whole truth about the Gospel, we're slowly discovering, comes not from any one mode alone but rather from the tension between them. And it's impossible to discover where to start in that tension unless you belong somewhere yourself. The most effective and committed ecumenists internationally are those who are also most solidly grounded and connected locally.

Objectivity then, against this background, for all its commendable components is not the most helpful conceptual model for the media in our day. There are alternatives that we've hardly begun to formulate. This book is our attempt to start the process of outlining them in the hope that other Christians will be encouraged to join in.

My own suggestion is that the marks of the alternative should include an unashamedly personal character, tested and disciplined by the fact that this personal expression is always made in the context of an open relationship with readers, viewers and listeners who can make their equally personal voices heard in reply.

I've also urged that an alternative concept should be holistic in nature, so that any one issue is approached from a variety of commitments, disciplines and backgrounds that together can do justice to the inter-relatedness of contemporary events and ideas. And finally I've suggested that any media assessment must involve a respect for Gospel scale, by which communication effectiveness is measured not so much in terms of sophisticated technology, capital investment, kilowatt power and circulation figures but also in terms of the depth, incisiveness and quality of its parable power, however small in size.

If an alternative concept was elaborated along these suggested lines it might well result in a more uneven media. But hopefully it would also be a more open media in which truth-telling was acknowledged to be a more fragile, complex and sometimes contradictory exercise than the orthodoxy of objectivity currently admits.

Of course, the possibility would remain that any new concept would be just as abused as the "objectivity" model we live with at present. No media concept, however theologically or philosophically sound, can act as a substitute for the courage, competence, care and personal honesty of the journalists and editors who have to make it work. For at the end of the day the practice of communication is a trade that depends on very basic skills and qualities and very severe practical limitations that church folk are often reluctant to recognize in their criticism. The next chapter will try to speak more pragmatically about these matters.

VIII. Making it happen

in which we argue that the last seven chapters aren't all high-altitude piety and offer some very down-to-earth distinctions and proposals that could enlist "other world" voices. The World Council of Churches' communication policy is used as a case study and the potential of church-related media is positively assessed. We end where the Gospel begins, with a call to repentance and a licence for muck-raking.

This is a book for people who are trying to cope with the media, who want to clarify their criticism of it and sort out what the Gospel has to say about it. The value of the exercise will depend on how effectively the arguments offered here can be interpreted and applied to your own local media — both secular and religious. Much of the material has evolved from my own involvement with church groups concerned about monitoring and challenging the effects of the media and trying to find more creative ways of communication.

Perhaps the single biggest weakness in such attempts is the lack of understanding and research about how the mass media actually works. This book can't remedy that lack except to argue that the first step in any media critique or any attempt to create an alternative form is face-to-face engagement with the journalists, editors or executives involved, around the sorts of questions suggested earlier on pages 10-11 and in Appendix II. Draw out the assumptions behind their editorial policy and find out what sort of people they are. If we can't begin by building our own critique within a context of personal relationships, then we can hardly expect others to respect such a context.

All our media meeting and relating may only serve to reveal just how imprisoned media people are in their orthodoxy, but it will ensure at least that our criticism is grounded in the way the media understands itself. And if we don't start there, we'll end up talking only to ourselves.

Such a starting point will immerse us almost immediately in the complexity of forms through which the mass media communicates. Our discussion to date has had to use the term "media" as a catch-all label. We haven't distinguished between one "medium" and another, nor even mentioned the exciting field of "group media" in which the variety of modern media are used together with traditional arts in small group settings.

But any criticism we make has to take account of the variety of functions and forms the blanket term "media" embraces. An information officer is not an investigative journalist, an evangelist doesn't have much in common with a news-room editor, though all four may claim media work in their job descriptions.

We need, then, to be very specific in our analysis about exactly what part of the media we're seeking to reform or replace, even though the same conceptual framework, attitudes and images often hold true across the whole range of media activity.

As our analysis builds up, there are several focal points that we'll have to keep returning to in our discussions. All have been introduced earlier, but in this more pragmatically orientated chapter, they deserve a second look.

The first is the old bug-a-boo of "objectivity". I've urged that this is not the most useful place to begin our media critique, and that it's smarter to build up the positive virtues of our alternative model rather than try a direct attack on the canons of media orthodoxy.

But confrontation on this issue there will inevitably be and when it comes, the strongest grounds to argue on may well be found by enlisting the aid of voices outside your local circle. For it's in the tension between third, second and first world self-understandings that the inadequacy of the western media's objectivity concept is most clearly revealed. And church people, with a worldwide ecumenical fellowship at their disposal, are especially well placed to invite the participation of "other world" voices in their local media debates. That participation will most certainly reveal that much of what First Worlders see as a perfectly innocent, neutral and straightforward account of events is seen by Third Worlders as a self-interested defence of the status quo.

Nowhere is this more clear than in the "objective" coverage of nuclear energy issues in western Europe and the US and the plea from advocates there for a halt to nuclear development, both peaceful and military. "But you've already got your nuclear power," is an increasingly common third world response, "and by demanding a halt in development now you're simply consolidating your own position."

With that suspicion lurking behind the debate, all the attempts at the objective beginnings are doomed to stalemate endings. The only way forward is through a style of interpretation that begins by taking full account of the vested interests and value commitments on both sides, and the political and economic contexts in which they see the issue. That way, we'll at least begin to see just how vast and firmly entrenched the nuclear industry is, and how difficult it is to debate nuclear ethics with any neutrality and detachment any more.

The second focal point that will probably draw protests of impractical piety is the frequent defence I've made of a more personal journalism, earthed in relationships and inviting response. That conviction has grown out of a couple of very practical encounters, quite apart from the strong biblical credentials that I see supporting the conviction.

The first is the strength of those communicators who anchor their work in the context of a community. The *Sojourners* magazine already referred to is one such enterprise — in which a magazine is published by a committed team who themselves form a multi-ministry community of service, worship and belief that readers are invited to share. To read the magazine is to get the sense that you have a stake in a larger human framework than that which is set by the printed page. If anything, the *Sojourners* media model succeeds too well in its relationship-centred style, for it often seems to be making demands of commitment from readers with an intensity that only living and praying together can sustain. Discipleship by post has its limitations.

But *Sojourners* is not the only example of this Gospel mark for the media. It's also evident in any publication that rises out of the heat of an experience in which readers are invited to share and sustain. Such media are often clumsily written, hastily assembled and cheaply printed, but that sort of provisionality is also a Gospel mark. The Kingdom, it seems, is still too far away from the present to rest easily on glossy paper, show up well in colour or reproduce clearly in stereophonic sound.

Apart from the success — at least on the Gospel's scale — of such small, community based, relationship-centred ventures, it's also clear that institution-based media are desperately in need of the same sort of strength. That's as clear for a body like the World Council of Churches as it is for any national or transnational denomination or corporation.

Despite its international, multi-media commitments, the WCC has yet to develop a communication strategy to match the complexity of its work. A largely ad hoc approach has relied on the products of professional communicators — the output of an "expert" and well-informed few who pass out material to a waiting constituency. A response is often invited but it's invariably seen as an auxiliary to the actual communication and not an essential part of that event. In that way the Council follows the approach of many of its member churches.

That sort of model is clearly inadequate as the sort of issues that the WCC attempts to communicate become more and more complex and multi-faceted, not only in their content, but also in the variety of audiences — first, second and third world, cultural and confessional — that 293 members churches in a 100 countries involve.

Somehow the Council has to evolve a new media model and at the 1978 meeting of its Communication Commission in Glion, Switzerland, a start was made in that process. The draft statement from that meeting is found in Appendix V and it at least opens the way to a more inclusive understanding of communication. Behind the statement is a real attempt to use the Gospel value judgments and commitments of the WCC as a base for defining communication policy, and to reflect those values in all their breadth and richness, rather than some "objective" ideal that the Council or the Gospel never pretends to have.

What the Glion statement also makes room for, but doesn't spell out, is that the WCC's communication task can no longer be seen simply as the responsibility of just a tiny and hopelessly overtaxed group of professionals whose expertise can never span the range of forms and skills required. If the Council forms an ecumenical community of churches as it claims, then the explanation and interpretation of ecumenical events has to be lodged and shared within that community. Communication would then be seen as the task of thousands rather than one Geneva-based department.

And if that is to happen then the media strategy must be towards informing, educating and equipping the thousands to do the job, preparing them beforehand with news and resources, listening to their responses and if necessary delaying or altering Council actions according to whether those actions can be adequately interpreted and understood by the network of communicators.

That way, the quality of the Council's communication becomes dependent on the quality of the Council's community. As the WCC monthly magazine *One World* says about its own health and survival:

However "successful" our promotion efforts are, *One World's* worth will not be finally expressed by our circulation figures or list of contents. Because the real nub of our value to the ecumenical movement lies in the quality of the community we build with and between our readers.

That such a community is bound to be tentative, more expectant than achieved, we readily acknowledge. Conversations through these pages will be hard to start and difficult to sustain across the cultural and spiritual chasms that separate Christians. We accept the assurance from the World Council's presidents in this issue that many churches know each other better, as an ecumenical fellowship, than ever before.

But better enough to sustain a magazine such as this? And if not, then with how much conviction can we ever affirm that the ecumenical movement makes a difference? Real flesh and blood differences in how we share and trust and sustain each other on a pilgrimage that the world declares to be a fool's dance anyway.

In that context, this magazine (and other ecumenical media) are acid tests of whether the ecumenical movement can still move, or whether we're trying to open the right doors with the wrong keys.

Perhaps the greatest single obstacle that we face in applying the arguments of this book to the mass media lies in the inevitably institutional character of the media itself. For how can you ever expect an institution, whether it be a government-controlled TV network or a church-controlled publication, to communicate in anything other than a self-interested way? Are the Presbyterians ever going to show the Methodists in a better light than themselves? Is the World Council ever going to admit to the mistakes it makes?

Most assessments of church media would answer such questions negatively. My own judgment is not so dismal. After ten years of working for Roman Catholic, Anglican, Methodist and now ecumenical publications, I've encountered enough signs of hope to believe that the established church is the one institution in modern society that has the mandate and the means to be able to demonstrate the sort of institutional openness that media credibility requires.

It might just be that the single most effective witness that the churches can make for a better "secular" mass media is to turn their own institutionally controlled "religious" media inside out and rely on the parable power of their action.

To do that, I believe, could open up wells of creativity that the church's media with rare exception simply doesn't believe exists. Whether we dare to tap those wells is bound up with our willingness to repent. For every effective act of communication depends on a prior act of confession.

The World Council of Churches was able to say nothing credible about the need for churches to disinvest in apartheid-reliant industry until it first demonstrated its conviction through its own investment portfolios.

A church with a membership unashamedly segregated by colour, culture or economic class speaks with faint voice on the subject of Christian community, no matter how cleverly worded its statements are. And all the talk about new economic orders falls on deaf ears unless we first admit our complicity and privilege under the present structures.

To make such admission in institutional terms will involve what David Jenkins described as Christian "muck-raking":

> Since the disturbances arising from the turbulence of the human situation throw into relief the inappropriate and often de-humanizing ways in which Christian operations and activities in fact operate, one of the most important lines of investigation related to setting the churches and their institutions free for greater contributions to being and becoming human is that which can perhaps be most forcibly described as "muck-raking". That is to say, rigorous and ruthless attention must be given to exposing those ways in which the churches are involved, and have accepted to be involved, in the sinful structures and practices of their conditioning societies. Everything from sanctifying societal patterns of male domination to unquestioned acceptance of the profits of exploitation must be laid open with as much honesty as possible.

> To be severely critical of an institution and its operations can be, certainly from a Christian viewpoint, a measure of commit-ment to the true being and purpose of that institution. It also has nothing directly to do with praise or blame. For a clear understanding of many institutional situations shows much more about men and women and being trapped than about their being worthy of praise or deserving of blame.

> Thus systematic Christian muck-raking could be a demon-stration of confidence in God, and a real commitment to justification by faith, which would lay open what is really required by way of repentance and freedom to contribute to the humanization of life.*

That stance of repentant openness in the media will involve heart-searching and pain. But it might bring us nearer to

---

* *The Humanum Studies 1969-1975*, pp. 70 and 83. Geneva: WCC, 1975.

speaking of life as it really is, and that after all, is an exercise that Christians need not fear. Let David Jenkins say why in a last word:

"The Incarnation of Jesus Christ declares to us that the nearer we come to reality the nearer we come to God, and that the more accurately we achieve an analysis of reality the more closely we come to suffering and sharing with God in his redemptive and creative work."

As a partner in that work, the media, whether church-sponsored or secular, takes on an exciting new potential. And the need for Christians to understand, evaluate and use the media creatively becomes more urgent than ever.

Appendices

APPENDIX I

ADVICE ON APPROACHING THE MEDIA

The following quotations are taken from "A guide to public relations planning" published by Air New Zealand's Public Affairs Department as a "practical aid to voluntary workers of community groups" and representative of much professional media advice. The paragraphs have been deliberately selected to illustrate the almost reverent attitude that the authors assume is desirable for best results in approaches to the media. The advice is a well-intended and very practical contribution to the groups concerned, but the unquestioning stance towards the media that is advocated here is nevertheless disturbing:

"Your organization's attitude at all times should be that you are endeavouring to provide useful, new information (in other words 'news') to the media, to the mutual benefit of the media and your organization. You should never have an attitude of trying to gain so-called 'free publicity'."

"You must recognize that it is a journalist's prerogative to arrive at his own evaluation of news. Obviously you will be disappointed if you have gone to some trouble to prepare a release and it is not used, or is heavily edited. But you will gain nothing by carping. Remember, they are professionals. Remember, too, that while your release seems extremely important to you, it is competing for space with hundreds and possibly thousands of other items."

" **'Bad' publicity**: Occasions may arise when media are seeking a story your organization would rather not see published. You must, on these and all occasions, recognize that your function is not to act as a block between the media and your organization. You are there to improve communications."

"Never resort to a flat 'no comment'. The media will dig out the facts anyway and you will have destroyed their confidence in you. Should the media wish to cover a story about your organization with its own staff, rather than use a release, welcome its approach and give all the assistance you can, such as background information and arranging interviews."

APPENDIX II

LOCAL EXERCISES IN MEDIA ANALYSIS

All these exercises need to be freely adapted to suit the needs of your group and situation. Hopefully they'll contain some hints for making your own media analysis more precise:

1. Make a list of the five most important events in the life of your community during the last month. State briefly what made them significant in your view, who benefitted most from them and who was instrumental in bringing them about.

Having completed your list, review how the local media covered the same five events and with what sort of prominence. At what points does your assessment differ from that provided by the media? What differences in value judgments are revealed by the comparison?

2. Invite a local editor to share with your group how he or she defines news and what sort of values are implied in the choice. Select beforehand a variety of different news stories (local and foreign) that received major and continuing attention and use them as test cases for the editor's definition. Find out the reasons why the stories you selected eventually stopped receiving publicity.

3. Gather a group of five or six people to discuss one current contentious issue in your local community and, working together, each prepare a response to that issue from different standpoints, e.g. legal, religious, historical, medical, etc. Then submit the responses in the form of letters to the editor, calls to radio talk-back shows or whatever other media access channels are open to you. Compare the treatment each perspective received — which angle did your media welcome, consider difficult to handle, find plainly unacceptable and why?

4. Select one very topical and prominent news story and compare the treatment it receives across the widest range of media available to you. Analyse which angles and details are consistently repeated or ignored. This is a revealing exercise even between two seemingly similar international news weeklies such as *Time* and *Newsweek*.

5. Invite representatives from minority group organizations (ethnic, political, religious) in your community to meet with you and share how adequately they believe their special cause is represented in the media. Discuss beforehand how well you yourselves believe their special interests and position are covered, then compare your judgment with that of the invited representatives.

6. Construct a chart of the most common impressions the media present of children, teenagers, women, old people, politicians, clergy, policemen and women, ethnic groups, housewives, business executives, military, etc. Are the images of any of these groups consistent? Stereotyped? Where are (positive or negative) moral judgments being made? Where have you been surprised and forced to reconsider your mental picture of any of these social or occupational groups?

7. Based on your own forecast, write your own version of some immediately impending events, locally or nationally. Then compare your version with the newspaper account when it comes. At what point

are your guesses confirmed? Where does the description and interpretation seem stereotyped? Are there any clues in the newspaper
account that lead you to doubt its accuracy and reliability?

8. Take one issue of a local newspaper and make a rough index of the
way space has been allocated to: local, national, international news;
first, second and third world concerns; advertising; economic, political,
religious, military issues; special interests of women, youth, married,
single, or elderly people; crime, romance, humour, etc. Other categories
will suggest themselves as you make your analysis. Having completed
the classification, ask who and what gets most attention and who and
what gets ignored. The newspaper holds up a mirror to society. How
does the image it presents compare with the reflection you believe to be
true?

APPENDIX III

SOME QUESTIONS ABOUT OBJECTIVE PHOTOGRAPHY

A statement from the World Council of Churches, Department of Communication, film and visual arts section, on the impossibility of objectivity in photography:

All photographs are partial. This comment runs counter to the generally accepted notion, which is: "It's true because I can see it."

In any photograph, the picture and the text illustrate the particular view of a particular photographer in a particular situation. All photographers are influenced by their own culture, way of life, education and training and will inevitably choose the picture which seems to reflect their own perception of a given situation. Their relationship to their subject, for example — respect, domination, etc. — their own position as an active agent external to the situation, the precise purpose for which a photograph is taken (financial gain, consciousness-raising, etc.) are all factors which make photographers' action in taking a photograph symptomatic.

1. Can a photographer, who is raised and trained in one culture, ever penetrate and understand another culture without distorting it?

2. Can a photograph ever be progressive in its content and reactionary in its form (in the sense that it lends itself to endless repetition, the reinforcement of stereotype and dominant ideologies)? As the form of any photo or artistic work runs the danger of being reactionary, how can we recognize and avoid this danger (for example, in photos of conferences taken for institutional record purposes)?

3. How can we avoid the dependency and domination contained in any photographer/subject relationship, especially in third world settings? Does the payment of a fee to the subject dissolve the problem?

4. Does a caption stating the conditions under which a photograph was produced (the culture, motivation, experience of the photographer, and how and why the particular subject was selected) make up for the photo's lack of reality?

APPENDIX IV

A CASE STUDY IN OBJECTIVE REPORTING

The following report appeared in the *New Zealand Herald* on 9 September 1975.

"Waste in Marriage"

Cohabitation and sex outside marriage should be socially acceptable for many people, a prominent Methodist minister said in Auckland yesterday.

Dr and Mrs H. J. Clinebell, touring New Zealand as guests of the New Zealand council of Christian social services, said on their arrival in Auckland that they believed the Bible was written for first-century Christians and was not applicable in modern society.

Dr Clinebell said that for many people the state of matrimony was not the most beneficial and, rather than allow resentment to grow and lead to a breakdown of the marriage, it should be socially acceptable for them to be able to cohabit.

"I believe social attitudes towards marriage are not as important as the ability to achieve an intimate relationship and to find love. Traditional ideas of matrimony are out of place in modern society," he said.

"Sex is an intense form of communication, and should only be practised under certain circumstances. I do not believe a state of matrimony is necessarily the right criterion, but rather it should be done as part of love, caring and commitment," he said.

There was a great waste to the world through marriage: many people felt trapped, and for this reason he felt that the more important factor was the happiness of the people concerned, rather than the traditional rules.

Mrs Clinebell said it was important for people to have the social freedom to discover their own "unique potential".

"Every person has some unique potential in life," she said. "This is as personal as your fingerprints, and it is usually only through counselling from others that this can be identified."

The Clinebells are specialists in marriage guidance counselling, and have written eight books on the topic. They have established counselling workshops in the main centres on a short tour of New Zealand.

Mrs Clinebell, a social worker, does not consider herself to be a Christian, but the two combine their different approaches in their teaching on their perfect-marriage formula.

Dr Clinebell said: "Theology and Christianity do not have much bearing on our teaching, but sometimes they help people towards an understanding of life, and are useful in filling value vacuums."

The Auckland district chairman of the Methodist Church, the Rev. E. D. Grounds, said last night that he did not feel the beliefs of Dr and Mrs Clinebell would reflect those of all Methodists or even all Christians.

"I would feel that while it is true the situation now may well be different from the time of the biblical writers," he said, "the principle underlying creation and the way we should live our lives remains the same."

The following correction appeared two days later. It goes into commendable detail and considerable length to satisfy the complaint, but could it be called an apology?

Methodist Couple Say Story Was Incorrect

A visiting American Methodist minister and his wife have claimed their views on marriage were distorted in a *Herald* article on Saturday.

Dr and Mrs H. J. Clinebell, who are touring New Zealand as guests of the New Zealand council of Christian social services, said yesterday parts of the article which appeared under the headline "Waste in Marriage" was neither what they said nor what they believed.

CONSTRUCTIVE

The Clinebells said: "The article suggests that we recommend cohabitation outside of marriage. What we said was that it is a fact that such relationships are increasingly common in many societies, that simply moralizing about it doesn't produce constructive results."

Instead the institutions of society, including the churches, needed to ask what were the harmful or constructive effects of sexual relationships on persons in any circumstances. Did a particular expression of human sexuality diminish or enhance our full personhood?

"It is our experience that sex tends to strengthen relationships when it occurs in a context of caring, mutual respect, love and commitment to each other's growth.

"Conversely, sex tends to hurt and diminish personhood when it occurs in a relationship of distrust and exploitation.

MORE CREATIVE

"Much sex outside marriage is destructive to the persons involved. But is is also true that much sex within marriage is dehumanizing and destructive," they said.

In their work, the couple said they had known of relationships not sanctioned by church or state that were both more creative and less exploitive than some marriage relationships.

"All of us who care about people need to be concerned with raising the general quality of human relationships, including the ways in which sex influences this quality."

Dr and Mrs Clinebell have just celebrated their 30th wedding anniversary and say they are committed to developing the most creative marriage they can.

The couple said the article claimed that Mrs Charlotte Clinebell "does not consider herself a Christian".

"That response by Charlotte was to the reporter's definition which equated being Christian with male dominance.

LIBERATION

"Such a definition seems to both of us to be neither Christian nor humanizing, but to reflect the patriarchal society of the first century which is no longer relevant. A Christian life-style is a humanizing life-style, as is true of any sound religious or humanistic approach to marriage.

"It affirms all human liberation movements in their demand for equality for everyone," they said.

The article also quoted the Clinebells as saying that "the Bible was written for first-century Christians and was not applicable in modern society".

To this they yesterday replied: "That is neither what we said nor what we believe. Howard (Dr Clinebell) suggested that the Bible is a goldmine of time-tested truths about life and constructive relationships which are relevant to our society.

"He also said that everything in a goldmine isn't gold. We should not confuse the sociological views of the first-century patriarchal society with inspired or relevant truths about life today."

INVALUABLE

The couple denied that Dr Clinebell had said "theology and Christianity do not have much bearing on our teachings..."

"He said that effective counselling is effective counselling regardless of who does it, and that there is no valid methodology called Christian counselling.

"He also said that theological and spiritual resources are invaluable in helping many people to cope..."

APPENDIX V

THE GLION COMMUNICATION GUIDELINES

A draft statement on policy guidelines from the World Council of Churches Communication Commission, at its March 1978 meeting, said:

The task of Christian communicators is to seek to tell the truth. The Christian understanding of that truth is admittedly complex and always incomplete. It is perceived in the message of the Bible, the person of Jesus, the tradition of the church, and contemporary events.

All these elements point to a God whose universal love contains a particular concern for the poor and the oppressed, and whose reconciling power embraces a passion for justice and freedom.

In commitment to that God, and in an attempt to reflect his truth, the World Council of Churches' policies call the churches towards unity, deeper renewal and sharing of spiritual experience and tradition, wider witness and greater service in the struggle against poverty, exploitation and oppression of every kind. Such commitment makes neutrality impossible.

These policies involve the Council's worldwide constituency, decision-making bodies and staff in value judgments and choices which are deliberately made and inevitably tension-creating. As a department of the WCC, the Communication Department works to provide the member churches and the wider public with information and interpretation of how these policies are conceived, and implemented and received. In so doing the department reflects the Council's decisions and shares in a common task.

Yet in its search for that same truth, and within the framework of the whole Council's commitment, the department requires a freedom, authority and initiative of its own, arising directly from its communication function and its responsibility to the member churches. Inherent in that function is a duty to share rather than suppress truth, to open rather than close the search.

Any freedom required by the department in order to discharge its task may sometimes be in tension with the diversity of ways in which its freedom is understood by the whole Council. The department must therefore ask that its freedom, authority and function be understood in terms of the whole *oikoumene* it seeks to serve. It must also ensure that its freedom is always exercised responsibly with the highest professional integrity and standards.

To foster this freedom to be responsible is in the best interest of the WCC. For in the end the Council's credibility depends on the openness with which it shares its information and the sensitivity (of tone and style) with which it speaks and listens to the *oikoumene* it serves.